The Story of Lacrosse

KJ Smith

To the Indigenous communities who first brought the spirit of lacrosse to life, and to the generations of players who have honored its legacy, skill, and intensity. This book is dedicated to those who play with respect, passion, and a commitment to the game's deep roots.

Contents

INTRODUCTION

Lacrosse, often referred to as "the fastest game on two feet," is a sport with deep historical roots and a rich cultural heritage. Originating among the Native American tribes of North America, lacrosse was more than just a game; it was a vital aspect of their social and spiritual lives. Known by various names such as "baggataway" or "the Creator's Game," lacrosse served as a means of resolving conflicts, training young warriors, and honoring the gods.

The story of lacrosse is a tale of transformation and adaptation. From its ancient beginnings, where hundreds of players competed on fields that stretched miles, to its modern incarnation with codified rules and international competitions, lacrosse has evolved significantly while maintaining its core essence. This sport, once confined to the indigenous communities of North America, has now spread across the globe, captivating the hearts and minds of players and fans from diverse backgrounds.

THE STORY OF LACROSSE

This book delves into the multifaceted history of lacrosse, tracing its journey from the sacred fields of Native American tribes to the professional arenas of today. We will explore how lacrosse was introduced to European settlers in the 17th century, how it was formalized and popularized in Canada and the United States, and how it eventually expanded to other parts of the world. Along the way, we will examine the significant changes in rules, equipment, and gameplay, as well as the development of women's lacrosse and the impact of legendary players and coaches.

Lacrosse's cultural and social significance cannot be understated. It has played a crucial role in community building, fostering a sense of identity and pride among its players and supporters. The sport's influence extends beyond the field, permeating movies, television, literature, fashion, and lifestyle. Moreover, the business of lacrosse, with its burgeoning professional leagues, media rights, sponsorships, and merchandising, showcases the sport's economic impact and growing popularity.

As we journey through the history of lacrosse, we will also address the social issues that the sport faces today, such as integration, inclusivity, and safety. By understanding the challenges and triumphs of lacrosse, we gain insight into its enduring appeal and its potential future trajectory.

Ultimately, this book celebrates lacrosse as a dynamic and unifying sport that transcends cultural and geographical boundaries. It is a testament to the game's resilience, adaptability, and the passion of those who play it. Join us as we uncover the captivating story of lacrosse, a sport that continues to inspire and unite people around the world.

ANCIENT BEGINNINGS

Lacrosse's origins are deeply intertwined with the history and culture of Native American tribes in North America. Known by various names such as "baggataway," "tewaarathon," or "the Creator's Game," lacrosse was more than just a sport; it was a vital aspect of the social, spiritual, and cultural fabric of Native American life. Its significance extended far beyond the physical competition, encompassing elements of religion, medicine, and community bonding.

The Role of Lacrosse in Native American Culture

Lacrosse was played by numerous tribes across the continent, including the Haudenosaunee (Iroquois), Cherokee, Choctaw, and many others. Each tribe had its own name for the game and its own variations in how it was played. Despite these differences, certain common elements and themes emerged, reflecting the deep cultural importance of the game.

For many tribes, lacrosse was considered a gift from the Creator, played for the pleasure of the gods and as a means of bringing people together. It was often used to settle disputes between tribes, acting as a peaceful alternative to war. The game was also believed to have medicinal properties, capable of healing the sick and ensuring the well-being of the community.

The spiritual significance of lacrosse was evident in the rituals and ceremonies that accompanied it. Games were often preceded by days of fasting, prayer, and dancing. Players would adorn themselves with special paint and feathers, and the wooden sticks and deerskin balls used in the game were crafted with great care and reverence.

Early Forms of the Game

Lacrosse games could involve hundreds of players and last for several days. Fields varied in size, sometimes stretching over miles of rugged terrain. The goals, usually marked by trees or poles, were often set at great distances apart. The objective was to carry or pass the ball into the opposing team's goal, using a stick with a netted pocket to catch, throw, and carry the ball.

The rules of the game were flexible and varied widely between tribes. In some versions, physical contact was minimal, while in others, it was an intense, full-contact sport. Protective gear was not commonly used, and injuries were frequent, adding to the game's reputation for toughness and endurance.

Despite the variations, the core elements of teamwork, skill, and strategy were always present. Players had to be adept at handling the stick and ball, as well as navigating the often rough and uneven playing fields. Speed, agility, and strength were highly prized attributes, and the best players were revered within their communities.

Regional Variations

Different regions developed their own unique styles and versions of lacrosse. For instance, the Haudenosaunee played a version of the game that emphasized long, high passes and teamwork, with each player having a specific role on the field. In contrast, the Cherokee played a more physical version known as "little brother of war," which was used to train young warriors and resolve conflicts.

The southeastern tribes, such as the Choctaw and Creek, played a variation of lacrosse called "stickball." This version used two sticks per player and had different rules and scoring methods. Stickball games were often held in conjunction with other community events, such as festivals and celebrations, highlighting the game's role in social cohesion.

Lacrosse and Community

Lacrosse was a unifying force within Native American communities. It brought together people of all ages and statuses, fostering a sense of camaraderie and shared purpose. The game was not just for the players; the entire community would gather to watch, cheer, and participate in the accompanying rituals and festivities.

Women also played a role in the cultural life of lacrosse, although they typically did not participate in the men's games. In some tribes, women had their own versions of the game or took on supportive roles, such as preparing food and organizing ceremonies.

The ancient beginnings of lacrosse reveal a game that was deeply embedded in the spiritual, social, and cultural life of Native American tribes. It was a multifaceted activity that went beyond mere sport, serving as a means of resolving conflicts, healing the sick, and uniting communities. As we explore the subsequent chapters, we will see how lacrosse evolved and adapted through the centuries, but its roots in Native American tradition remain a foundational aspect of its enduring legacy.

LACROSSE AND COLONIAL AMERICA

As European settlers arrived in North America in the 17th century, they encountered a game that was both fascinating and foreign to them: lacrosse. This chapter explores the early interactions between Native Americans and Europeans involving lacrosse, the introduction of the game to colonial communities, and its gradual spread throughout the continent.

Early Encounters

The first documented European encounters with lacrosse occurred in the early 1600s, when French Jesuit missionaries observed Native American tribes playing the game. The Jesuits were intrigued by the sport, noting its intensity, the skill of the players, and its cultural significance. In their writings, they described the game in detail, providing some of the earliest recorded accounts of lacrosse.

One of the most notable observers was Jean de Brébeuf, a Jesuit missionary who lived among the Huron tribe in the 1630s. He was the first to use the term "lacrosse" to describe the game, drawing a parallel between the shape of the stick and a bishop's crosier (la crosse in French). Brébeuf's accounts highlighted the communal and spiritual aspects of the game, as well as its role in physical training and conflict resolution.

Introduction to European Settlers

As European settlers began to establish colonies in North America, they were gradually introduced to lacrosse by Native Americans. These interactions were often informal, with settlers observing or occasionally participating in the game. Lacrosse served as a cultural bridge, providing a means for Native Americans and Europeans to engage with one another outside of the more hostile and contentious aspects of colonization.

In some instances, Native Americans used lacrosse as a diplomatic tool, organizing matches to welcome or entertain European visitors. These games allowed for a peaceful exchange of cultures and demonstrated the athletic prowess and organizational skills of the Native American players. The settlers, in turn, were often impressed by the game's speed, physicality, and the high level of skill required to play it.

The Spread of Lacrosse

The spread of lacrosse among colonial communities was gradual but steady. European settlers who had witnessed the game began to adopt and adapt it, incorporating elements of lacrosse into their recreational activities. This early adoption was most prominent in areas with significant Native American populations, such as the Great Lakes region and the northeastern United States.

In these regions, lacrosse began to evolve as settlers made modifications to suit their own preferences and circumstances. The fields were often smaller, the number of players reduced, and the rules simplified. These adaptations made the game more accessible to settlers, who were not as familiar with the traditional Native American versions of lacrosse.

Cultural Exchange and Transformation

Lacrosse became a symbol of the broader cultural exchange occurring between Native Americans and European settlers. While the game retained many of its traditional elements, it also underwent significant transformations. European settlers introduced new materials and techniques, such as using leather for the ball and adopting different stick-making methods. These changes contributed to the game's evolution and helped bridge the gap between Native American and European practices.

The cultural exchange was not without its tensions, however. As settlers increasingly encroached on Native American lands and imposed their own ways of life, the traditional practices and significance of lacrosse were sometimes overshadowed or misunderstood. Nonetheless, the game's resilience and adaptability allowed it to survive and thrive in this new context.

Lacrosse in Colonial Communities

By the late 18th century, lacrosse had become a fixture in some colonial communities, particularly in Canada. The game was played informally among settlers and Native Americans alike, fostering a sense of shared identity and community. In these early colonial lacrosse matches, the spirit of cooperation and mutual respect was often evident, reflecting the game's origins as a tool for diplomacy and unity.

Lacrosse's integration into colonial life also laid the groundwork for its future development and formalization. As the game continued to gain popularity, it would eventually attract the attention of individuals who would seek to standardize and promote it on a larger scale, setting the stage for lacrosse's modern era.

The story of lacrosse in colonial America is one of cultural encounter and adaptation. Introduced to European settlers by Native Americans, the game served as a means of bridging cultural divides and fostering mutual understanding. Despite the challenges and changes brought by colonization, lacrosse retained its core essence and continued to evolve, spreading throughout colonial communities and laying the foundation for its future growth. As we move forward in the history of lacrosse, we will see how these early interactions and adaptations set the stage for the formalization and popularization of the game in the 19th century.

FORMALIZING THE GAME

The mid-19th century marked a pivotal period in the history of lacrosse, as the game underwent significant changes and began to take on a more structured and organized form. This chapter explores the role of Dr. William George Beers in modernizing lacrosse, the establishment of the Montreal Lacrosse Club, the codification of rules, and the formation of organized leagues that laid the groundwork for the sport as we know it today.

The Role of Dr. William George Beers

Dr. William George Beers, often referred to as the "father of modern lacrosse," was a pivotal figure in the formalization and promotion of the game. A Canadian dentist and passionate lacrosse player, Beers recognized the potential of lacrosse to become a widely popular and organized sport. He dedicated himself to modernizing the game, making it more accessible and appealing to a broader audience.

In the 1860s, Beers began his efforts to standardize lacrosse rules and equipment. He believed that a formalized set of rules was essential for the game's growth and legitimacy. To this end, he wrote and published the first official rulebook for lacrosse in 1867, titled "Lacrosse: The National Game of Canada." This rulebook laid the foundation for the standardized version of the game, establishing guidelines for gameplay, equipment, and field dimensions.

The Establishment of the Montreal Lacrosse Club

The Montreal Lacrosse Club, founded in 1856, played a crucial role in the development and popularization of lacrosse. It was one of the first organized lacrosse clubs in Canada and served as a hub for players and enthusiasts to come together and promote the sport. The club hosted regular matches and tournaments, attracting significant attention and helping to elevate the profile of lacrosse.

The Montreal Lacrosse Club also became a center for innovation and refinement of the game. Club members, including Dr. Beers, experimented with different rules and equipment, seeking to improve the sport's safety and enjoyment. These efforts contributed to the game's evolution and helped establish Montreal as a key center for lacrosse in Canada.

Codifying the Rules

The codification of lacrosse rules by Dr. Beers was a major milestone in the sport's history. His rulebook provided a clear and consistent framework for how the game should be played, addressing key aspects such as:

- Field Dimensions: Beers standardized the size of the lacrosse field, making it more uniform and manageable.
- Number of Players: The rulebook specified the number of players on each team, typically twelve, to ensure a balanced and organized game.
- Equipment: Guidelines for sticks, balls, and protective gear were established, improving player safety and standardizing gameplay.
- Gameplay Rules: Beers outlined the basic rules of play, including how goals were scored, penalties, and the roles of different positions on the field.

These standardized rules made it easier for new players to learn and enjoy the game, and they facilitated the organization of official matches and tournaments.

The Formation of Organized Leagues

With standardized rules in place, lacrosse began to see the formation of organized leagues and associations. One of the earliest and most significant was the National Lacrosse Association of Canada, founded in 1867. This organization brought together various lacrosse clubs and teams from across Canada, providing a structured framework for competition and promoting the sport on a national level.

The establishment of leagues and associations helped to formalize the competitive aspect of lacrosse, introducing regular seasons, championships, and inter-club matches. These developments attracted more players and spectators, further boosting the sport's popularity and visibility.

Early Matches and Tournaments

The first recorded matches under the newly standardized rules took place in the late 1860s and early 1870s. These matches were often high-profile events, drawing large crowds and media attention. One notable early match was the game between the Montreal Lacrosse Club and the Toronto Cricket Club in 1867, which showcased the sport's growing appeal and competitive spirit.

Tournaments also began to emerge as key events in the lacrosse calendar. The Dominion Lacrosse Tournament, first held in 1867, brought together teams from across Canada to compete for national honors. These tournaments provided a platform for showcasing talent, fostering rivalries, and promoting the sport to a wider audience.

The mid-19th century was a transformative period for lacrosse, as the efforts of individuals like Dr. William George Beers and organizations like the Montreal Lacrosse Club helped to formalize and popularize the game. The codification of rules, the establishment of organized leagues, and the hosting of early matches and tournaments laid the foundation for lacrosse's evolution into a modern, structured sport. As we continue to explore the history of lacrosse, we will see how these early developments set the stage for the game's growth and expansion in Canada, the United States, and beyond.

GROWTH IN CANADA & THE UNITED STATES

The late 19th and early 20th centuries saw lacrosse flourish in Canada and expand significantly into the United States. This chapter examines the sport's rise in popularity in both countries, the founding of key organizations, the role of colleges and universities in promoting the game, and the cultural impact of lacrosse during this period.

Lacrosse's Rise in Popularity in Canada

Following the formalization of the game's rules and the establishment of organized leagues, lacrosse quickly became one of Canada's most popular sports. The National Lacrosse Association of Canada, founded in 1867, played a pivotal role in promoting the sport nationwide. The association organized tournaments, facilitated inter-club matches, and helped standardize the rules, fostering a competitive and vibrant lacrosse community.

By the late 19th century, lacrosse had become deeply embedded in Canadian culture. The sport was particularly popular in Quebec and Ontario, where numerous clubs and teams competed regularly. Lacrosse matches drew large crowds, and the sport was often featured in newspapers and magazines, further enhancing its visibility and appeal.

The establishment of the Montreal Shamrocks and the Toronto Lacrosse Club as dominant teams in the late 1800s exemplified the high level of competition and skill in Canadian lacrosse. These teams, along with others, helped elevate the sport's status and set the standard for excellence in play.

The Founding of the National Lacrosse Association of Canada

The National Lacrosse Association of Canada (NLAC) was instrumental in organizing and promoting the sport at a national level. The association's efforts to standardize rules and facilitate competitions provided a structured framework for the growth of lacrosse. The NLAC also played a key role in fostering a sense of community and shared identity among players and fans.

One of the association's significant contributions was the creation of the Minto Cup in 1901, a trophy awarded annually to the top senior amateur lacrosse team in Canada.

The Minto Cup quickly became one of the most prestigious awards in Canadian lacrosse, symbolizing the highest level of achievement in the sport.

Expansion to American Colleges and Universities

Lacrosse's expansion into the United States was significantly influenced by the sport's adoption by American colleges and universities. The first recorded lacrosse game in the United States took place in 1877, when New York University played against Manhattan College. This match marked the beginning of a broader movement to introduce lacrosse to American educational institutions.

By the early 20th century, lacrosse had established a strong presence in many American colleges and universities, particularly in the northeastern United States. Institutions such as Johns Hopkins University, Harvard University, and the University of Maryland became early adopters and advocates of the sport. These schools formed the foundation of American collegiate lacrosse, setting the stage for the sport's growth and development in the United States.

The formation of the United States Intercollegiate Lacrosse Association (USILA) in 1882 further facilitated the sport's expansion. The USILA organized intercollegiate competitions, established rules and standards, and promoted lacrosse as a key component of American college athletics. The association's efforts helped elevate the status of lacrosse, attracting talented athletes and fostering a competitive spirit among college teams.

Lacrosse and American Culture

As lacrosse gained popularity in the United States, it began to influence American culture in various ways. The sport's fast-paced, physical nature appealed to American sensibilities, and its emphasis on teamwork and strategy resonated with the values of collegiate athletics. Lacrosse matches became social events, drawing large crowds and creating a sense of community among players and fans.

The media also played a significant role in promoting lacrosse. Newspapers and magazines covered games, profiled star players, and highlighted the sport's unique attributes. This increased visibility helped generate interest and enthusiasm for lacrosse, contributing to its growing popularity.

Key Figures and Teams

Several key figures and teams emerged during this period, shaping the trajectory of lacrosse in Canada and the United States. In Canada, players like George "Sport" Sweeney and teams like the Montreal Shamrocks became legends of the game, setting records and achieving significant milestones. Their contributions helped elevate the sport's status and inspired future generations of lacrosse players.

In the United States, pioneers such as Roscoe Brown and teams like the Johns Hopkins Blue Jays played crucial roles in promoting and developing lacrosse. These individuals and teams set high standards for play, demonstrated the sport's potential, and laid the groundwork for lacrosse's future growth.

The late 19th and early 20th centuries were a period of significant growth and expansion for lacrosse in Canada and the United States. The sport's rise in popularity, the establishment of key organizations, and the influence of colleges and universities helped solidify lacrosse's place in North American culture. As we continue to explore the history of lacrosse, we will see how these early developments paved the way for further evolution and international expansion in the decades to come.

THE EVOLUTION OF THE GAME

The evolution of lacrosse throughout the 20th century was marked by significant changes in rules, equipment, and gameplay. This chapter delves into these transformations, the introduction of field lacrosse and box lacrosse, and the innovations in strategies and techniques that have shaped the modern game.

Changes in Rules

As lacrosse continued to grow in popularity, the need for standardized rules became increasingly important. The early 20th century saw several revisions to the rules to make the game safer, more consistent, and more appealing to a broader audience. Some key changes included:

- Standardized Field Dimensions: The dimensions of the lacrosse field were standardized to create a uniform playing surface. This included specifying the size and placement of goals, as well as the boundaries of the playing area.

- Player Positions and Numbers: The rules were refined to clearly define player positions and the number of players on each team. This helped to create a more organized and strategic game.
- Penalties and Fouls: A formalized system for penalties and fouls was introduced to ensure fair play and player safety. This included the establishment of penalty boxes and specific consequences for different infractions.

These changes helped to professionalize lacrosse, making it more accessible and enjoyable for players and fans alike.

Equipment Innovations

Advancements in technology and materials led to significant improvements in lacrosse equipment throughout the 20th century. Early lacrosse sticks were made from wood and were relatively rudimentary in design. As the game evolved, so did the equipment:

- Sticks: The introduction of aluminum and composite materials revolutionized lacrosse sticks, making them lighter, stronger, and more durable. The shape and design of the stick head also evolved, allowing for better ball control and accuracy.

- Protective Gear: As the game became more physical, the development of protective gear became crucial. Helmets, gloves, shoulder pads, and arm guards were introduced and continually improved to enhance player safety.
- Footwear: Specialized lacrosse cleats were developed to provide better traction and support on the field, improving players' speed and agility.

These equipment innovations not only enhanced player performance but also contributed to the overall growth and professionalism of the sport.

Introduction of Field Lacrosse and Box Lacrosse

The 20th century saw the emergence of two distinct forms of lacrosse: field lacrosse and box lacrosse. Each variant brought its own unique characteristics and appeal:

- Field Lacrosse: Field lacrosse, played on an outdoor field, remained true to the traditional format of the game. It emphasized speed, strategy, and teamwork, with a focus on long passes, quick transitions, and coordinated plays. Field lacrosse became particularly popular in North American colleges and universities, where it thrived as a competitive sport.

- Box Lacrosse: Box lacrosse, also known as indoor lacrosse, emerged in the 1930s in Canada. Played in a hockey rink-sized arena with a smaller goal and fewer players, box lacrosse was a faster, more intense version of the game. It emphasized close-quarters play, quick passes, and physicality. Box lacrosse quickly gained popularity in Canada and led to the formation of professional leagues.

Both forms of lacrosse contributed to the sport's diversification and allowed it to reach new audiences. The coexistence of field and box lacrosse provided players with different styles of play and expanded the sport's cultural footprint.

Innovations in Strategies and Techniques

As lacrosse evolved, so did the strategies and techniques employed by players and teams. Coaches and players continually sought ways to gain a competitive edge, leading to several key innovations:

- Offensive Strategies: Teams developed more sophisticated offensive plays, including set plays, pick-and-rolls, and coordinated attacks. The use of motion offenses and off-ball movement became critical to creating scoring opportunities.
- Defensive Tactics: Defensive strategies also evolved, with teams employing zone defenses, man-to-man coverage, and double teams to stifle opponents' attacks. The role of the goalie became more

specialized, with advanced techniques for shot-stopping and clearing the ball.

- Face-Off Techniques: The face-off, a critical aspect of lacrosse, saw significant innovations. Players developed specialized techniques to gain possession of the ball quickly and effectively, leading to the emergence of face-off specialists.

These strategic and technical advancements enhanced the overall quality of play and made lacrosse a more dynamic and exciting sport.

The evolution of lacrosse throughout the 20th century was characterized by significant changes in rules, equipment, and gameplay. The introduction of field lacrosse and box lacrosse provided players and fans with diverse experiences, while innovations in strategies and techniques elevated the sport's level of competition. As we continue to explore the history of lacrosse, we will see how these developments paved the way for the sport's continued growth and international expansion in the modern era.

LACROSSE IN THE 20TH CENTURY

The 20th century was a transformative period for lacrosse, marked by its establishment as a major sport in North America, the development of key teams and players, and the formation of professional leagues. This chapter examines the role of lacrosse in early 20th-century sports culture, highlights significant teams and players, and explores the establishment of professional lacrosse leagues.

Early 20th-Century Sports Culture

In the early 20th century, lacrosse cemented its place in the sports culture of North America, particularly in Canada and the United States. The sport was embraced by communities for its fast-paced and physical nature, and it was often seen as a symbol of cultural pride and identity.

Lacrosse matches became significant social events, drawing large crowds and fostering a sense of community. Schools, colleges, and local clubs played a crucial role in promoting the sport, with intercollegiate and interscholastic competitions becoming increasingly popular. These matches not only provided entertainment but also helped to develop young talent and foster a sense of teamwork and sportsmanship.

Key Teams and Players

The early 20th century saw the emergence of several key teams and legendary players who left an indelible mark on the sport. In Canada, the Montreal Shamrocks and the Toronto Tecumsehs were dominant forces, consistently performing at high levels and winning numerous championships. Their fierce rivalry captivated fans and contributed to the sport's popularity.

In the United States, teams like the Johns Hopkins Blue Jays and the University of Maryland Terrapins became powerhouses in collegiate lacrosse. Their successes in intercollegiate competitions helped to elevate the status of lacrosse and inspire other institutions to invest in the sport.

Several players from this era became icons in the lacrosse world. One of the most notable figures was Jim Brown, who is widely regarded as one of the greatest athletes of all time. Brown's exceptional skill, speed, and physicality made him a standout player at Syracuse University, where he earned All-American honors in both lacrosse and football. His success on the lacrosse field, coupled with his later achievements in professional football, helped to raise the profile of the sport.

Another legendary player was Gaylord Powless, a member of the Mohawk Nation, who was known for his exceptional stick skills and strategic mind. Powless played a crucial role in promoting lacrosse within Indigenous communities and served as an inspiration for future generations of players.

The Establishment of Professional Lacrosse Leagues

The latter half of the 20th century saw the establishment of professional lacrosse leagues, which played a significant role in the sport's development and commercialization. The formation of these leagues provided a platform for elite players to compete at the highest level and helped to elevate the sport's visibility and legitimacy.

- National Lacrosse League (NLL): The NLL, established in 1986, is one of the most prominent professional lacrosse leagues in North America. Initially focused on indoor lacrosse (box lacrosse), the NLL has grown to include teams from both the United States and Canada. The league's success is attributed to its high level of competition, strong fan base, and effective marketing strategies. The NLL has also played a crucial role in promoting the sport to new audiences and fostering the development of young talent.

- Major League Lacrosse (MLL): Founded in 2001, the MLL was the first professional field lacrosse league in the United States. The league aimed to showcase the best field lacrosse talent and provide a platform for the sport's growth. The MLL introduced several innovations, including a faster-paced game and a two-point scoring system, which added excitement and attracted fans. The league's establishment marked a significant milestone in the professionalization of field lacrosse.

Major Tournaments and Championships

The 20th century also saw the establishment of several major tournaments and championships that became key fixtures in the lacrosse calendar. These events provided opportunities for the best teams and players to compete at the highest level and showcased the sport's growth and development.

- NCAA Lacrosse Championship: The NCAA Lacrosse Championship, first held in 1971, quickly became one of the most prestigious events in collegiate lacrosse. The tournament brought together the best college teams from across the United States to compete for the national title. The championship's popularity and high level of competition helped to elevate the status of collegiate lacrosse and inspire young athletes to pursue the sport.

- Minto Cup and Mann Cup: In Canada, the Minto Cup (for junior teams) and the Mann Cup (for senior teams) became the most coveted trophies in box lacrosse. These tournaments showcased the best amateur and senior lacrosse talent in the country and played a crucial role in promoting the sport at various levels.

The 20th century was a period of significant growth and development for lacrosse. The sport became firmly established in North American sports culture, with key teams and players leaving a lasting legacy. The establishment of professional leagues and major tournaments provided a platform for elite competition and helped to elevate the sport's visibility and legitimacy. As we continue to explore the history of lacrosse, we will see how these developments set the stage for the sport's international expansion and continued evolution in the 21st century.

INTERNATIONAL EXPANSION

The late 20th and early 21st centuries witnessed lacrosse expanding beyond its North American roots to gain popularity and establish a presence in various countries around the world. This chapter examines the spread of lacrosse to countries such as England, Australia, and Japan, the formation of the Federation of International Lacrosse (FIL), and the significance of major international competitions like the World Lacrosse Championship.

The Spread of Lacrosse to Other Countries

Lacrosse's international journey began with the efforts of enthusiasts and expatriates who introduced the game to new regions. Several key milestones marked the sport's global expansion:

- England: Lacrosse was introduced to England in the 19th century, primarily through the influence of

Canadian expatriates. The game gained traction in British schools and universities, with clubs forming across the country. The English Lacrosse Association (ELA) was founded in 1892, and the sport has since maintained a strong presence, particularly among women's teams.

- Australia: Lacrosse arrived in Australia in the late 19th century, brought by Canadian gold miners and other expatriates. The first recorded game in Australia took place in 1876 in Melbourne. The sport quickly spread to other cities, and by the early 20th century, organized competitions and leagues were established. The Australian Lacrosse Association (ALA) was formed in 1931, solidifying the sport's presence.

- Japan: Lacrosse was introduced to Japan in the 1980s, primarily through exchange programs and international students. The sport quickly gained popularity, particularly in universities. The Japan Lacrosse Association (JLA) was founded in 1987, and Japan has since developed competitive men's and women's teams that participate in international competitions.

- Other Regions: Lacrosse also spread to other regions, including Europe, Asia, and Africa, driven by the efforts of expatriates, exchange programs, and international tournaments. Countries like Germany, Scotland, Ireland, South Korea, and Uganda have all seen the establishment of lacrosse teams and associations, contributing to the sport's global growth.

Formation of the Federation of International Lacrosse (FIL)

The Federation of International Lacrosse (FIL) was established in 2008 through the merger of the International Lacrosse Federation (ILF) and the International Federation of Women's Lacrosse Associations (IFWLA). The formation of the FIL marked a significant step towards unifying the sport under a single governing body and promoting its development on a global scale.

The FIL's mission is to foster the growth and development of lacrosse worldwide, promote fair play and sportsmanship, and organize international competitions. The organization has played a crucial role in standardizing rules, facilitating communication between national associations, and supporting emerging lacrosse programs in new regions.

Major International Competitions

International competitions have been instrumental in showcasing the sport's global appeal and providing a platform for the best teams and players to compete. Several key tournaments have become fixtures in the international lacrosse calendar:

- World Lacrosse Championship: The World Lacrosse Championship, organized by the FIL, is the premier international competition for men's lacrosse. The tournament, first held in 1967, brings together national teams from around the world to compete for the title of world champion. The event has grown significantly over the years, with the 2018 championship featuring 46 teams from five continents.

- Women's Lacrosse World Cup: The Women's Lacrosse World Cup, also organized by the FIL, is the equivalent competition for women's lacrosse. The tournament, first held in 1982, showcases the best women's teams globally and has played a crucial role in promoting and developing women's lacrosse.

- U19 World Lacrosse Championships: The FIL also organizes U19 World Lacrosse Championships for both men and women, providing a platform for young talent to compete at the highest level. These tournaments help to identify and nurture the next generation of lacrosse stars.

- European Lacrosse Championship: The European

Lacrosse Federation (ELF) organizes the European Lacrosse Championship, which brings together national teams from across Europe. The tournament, first held in 1995, has contributed to the growth of lacrosse in Europe and helped to raise the standard of competition in the region.

Growth and Development of Lacrosse Programs

The global expansion of lacrosse has been supported by the establishment of national associations and development programs aimed at promoting the sport at the grassroots level. These initiatives have been crucial in introducing lacrosse to new regions and providing opportunities for young players to learn and enjoy the game.

- Coaching and Development Programs: Many national associations, with support from the FIL, have implemented coaching and development programs to train coaches, officials, and players. These programs help to build a solid foundation for the sport's growth and ensure that new players receive quality instruction.

- International Friendlies and Exchange Programs: International friendlies and exchange programs have facilitated cultural exchange and provided valuable competitive experience for teams. These initiatives have helped to strengthen ties between lacrosse communities worldwide and promote the sport's values of teamwork and sportsmanship.

- Lacrosse for Development: In some regions, lacrosse has been used as a tool for social development and community building. Programs in countries like Uganda have demonstrated how lacrosse can provide opportunities for education, personal growth, and community engagement.

The international expansion of lacrosse has transformed the sport from a North American pastime into a global phenomenon. The efforts of enthusiasts, the formation of the Federation of International Lacrosse, and the establishment of major international competitions have all contributed to this remarkable growth. As we continue to explore the history of lacrosse, we will see how these developments have paved the way for the sport's continued evolution and the emergence of new lacrosse communities around the world.

WOMEN'S LACROSSE

The evolution and growth of women's lacrosse is a significant chapter in the history of the sport. Women's lacrosse has developed its own unique style, rules, and culture, and has seen substantial growth in participation and popularity over the past century. This chapter explores the development of women's lacrosse, the key early figures who contributed to its rise, the differences in rules and equipment between men's and women's lacrosse, and the growth of women's leagues and international competitions.

The Development of Women's Lacrosse

Women's lacrosse has roots dating back to the early 20th century, with its origins closely tied to the sport's introduction in British and American schools. Unlike the men's game, which evolved from traditional Native American lacrosse, women's lacrosse was developed as a distinct sport with its own set of rules and style of play.

The first recorded women's lacrosse game took place in 1890 at St. Leonard's School in St. Andrews, Scotland. The school's headmistress, Louisa Lumsden, played a crucial role in introducing and promoting the sport among young women. She had witnessed a men's lacrosse game in Canada and believed that a version of the sport would be suitable for her students. The game quickly gained popularity in British schools and soon spread to women's colleges in the United States.

Key Early Figures

Several key figures were instrumental in the development and promotion of women's lacrosse:

- Rosabelle Sinclair: Known as the "mother of women's lacrosse" in the United States, Rosabelle Sinclair was a Scottish educator who brought the sport to the Bryn Mawr School in Baltimore, Maryland, in 1926. She established the first women's lacrosse team in the United States and was a strong advocate for the sport, helping to spread it to other schools and colleges.

- Constance Applebee: Another significant figure in the history of women's lacrosse, Constance Applebee was an English physical education teacher who introduced the sport to women's colleges in the

United States in the early 1900s. She founded the first women's lacrosse teams at Vassar College and Wellesley College and played a key role in the development of the sport's rules and regulations.

- Margery Fish: A pioneer in British women's lacrosse, Margery Fish was a leading player and advocate for the sport in the early 20th century. She helped to organize the first international women's lacrosse match between England and Scotland in 1913, which marked a significant milestone in the sport's development.

Differences in Rules and Equipment

Women's lacrosse has distinct differences from men's lacrosse, reflecting its unique history and emphasis on skill and finesse over physical contact:

- Rules: Women's lacrosse rules are designed to minimize physical contact and emphasize skillful stick handling and passing. Body checking is not allowed, and stick checking must be controlled and directed away from the opponent's body. The field is typically larger, and there are fewer players on the field compared to men's lacrosse.

- Equipment: The equipment used in women's lacrosse is different from that used in men's lacrosse.

Women's lacrosse players use lighter sticks with shallower pockets, which require more precise handling and control. Protective gear is also minimal, with players typically wearing only goggles and mouthguards, reflecting the non-contact nature of the game.

Growth of Women's Leagues and International Competitions

The growth of women's lacrosse has been marked by the establishment of leagues and international competitions that have helped to raise the profile of the sport and provide opportunities for women to compete at the highest level:

- Collegiate Leagues: Women's lacrosse has become a major sport in American colleges and universities, with the NCAA Women's Lacrosse Championship being one of the most prestigious competitions. The first NCAA Women's Lacrosse Championship was held in 1982, and the tournament has since grown in size and popularity, attracting top talent from across the country.

- Professional Leagues: In recent years, professional women's lacrosse leagues have been established, providing a platform for elite players to compete beyond college. The Women's Professional Lacrosse

League (WPLL), founded in 2018, and the Athletes Unlimited Lacrosse League, launched in 2021, have both played significant roles in promoting and developing women's professional lacrosse.

- International Competitions: The Women's Lacrosse World Cup, organized by the Federation of International Lacrosse (FIL), is the premier international competition for women's lacrosse. The tournament, first held in 1982, brings together national teams from around the world to compete for the title of world champion. The World Cup has grown in size and prestige, showcasing the best talent and fostering the sport's global development.

- Youth and Club Leagues: The growth of youth and club leagues has also contributed to the development of women's lacrosse. These leagues provide opportunities for young players to learn the game, develop their skills, and compete in organized competitions. Grassroots initiatives and development programs have been crucial in expanding the sport's reach and increasing participation among girls and women.

The development and growth of women's lacrosse is a testament to the passion and dedication of its early pioneers and the many players, coaches, and advocates who have worked tirelessly to promote the sport. Women's lacrosse has evolved into a dynamic and competitive sport with its own unique identity, rules, and culture. As we continue to explore the history of lacrosse, we will see how the contributions of women's lacrosse have enriched the sport and helped to shape its future.

ICONIC PLAYERS AND COACHES

The history of lacrosse is adorned with the achievements of iconic players and coaches whose contributions have left an indelible mark on the sport. This chapter profiles some of the most legendary figures in lacrosse, including Jim Brown, Gary Gait, and Paul Rabil, explores the influence of pioneering coaches, and highlights the Lacrosse Hall of Fame and its notable inductees.

Legendary Players

Lacrosse has been graced by many exceptional players who have set records, won championships, and inspired future generations. Here are profiles of a few of the most legendary players in the history of the sport:

- Jim Brown: Widely considered one of the greatest athletes of all time, Jim Brown's impact on lacrosse is profound. Before becoming an NFL legend, Brown was a standout lacrosse player at Syracuse University in the 1950s. His combination of size, speed, and skill made him nearly unstoppable on the lacrosse field. Brown's excellence in both lacrosse and football has made him an enduring icon and a symbol of athletic versatility.

- Gary Gait: Gary Gait is often hailed as the greatest lacrosse player of all time. Born in Victoria, British Columbia, Gait, along with his twin brother Paul, revolutionized the sport in the late 1980s and 1990s. At Syracuse University, Gary Gait was a three-time All-American and led the Orange to three NCAA championships. Known for his innovative playing style, including the famous "Air Gait" move, Gait's influence extended to professional lacrosse, where he enjoyed a highly successful career in both the National Lacrosse League (NLL) and Major League Lacrosse (MLL).

- Paul Rabil: A modern lacrosse superstar, Paul Rabil is renowned for his incredible athleticism and scoring prowess. Rabil played collegiate lacrosse at Johns Hopkins University, where he won two NCAA championships. His professional career has been equally impressive, with multiple MVP awards and championships in both the MLL and NLL. Rabil's dedication to growing the sport led him to co-found the Premier Lacrosse League (PLL) in 2018, which has quickly become one of the premier professional lacrosse leagues in the world.

Influential Coaches

Coaches have played a pivotal role in shaping the sport of lacrosse, developing strategies, and mentoring players. Several coaches stand out for their contributions to the game:

-   Dave Pietramala: A legendary coach and former player, Dave Pietramala is synonymous with success in collegiate lacrosse. As a player, he was a dominant defenseman at Johns Hopkins University, winning the Schmeisser Award as the nation's top defenseman twice. As a coach, Pietramala led Johns Hopkins to two NCAA championships and numerous Final Four appearances. His defensive strategies and emphasis on discipline have left a lasting impact on the sport.

-   Bill Tierney: Bill Tierney is one of the most successful coaches in lacrosse history, known for his ability to build winning programs. He led Princeton University to six NCAA championships, transforming the Tigers into a lacrosse powerhouse. Tierney later took over the University of Denver's program, leading the Pioneers to their first NCAA championship in 2015, making them the first team west of the Mississippi River to win the title. Tierney's innovative coaching methods and recruitment strategies have greatly influenced the sport.

- Cindy Timchal: A trailblazer in women's lacrosse, Cindy Timchal is the winningest coach in NCAA Division I women's lacrosse history. She led the University of Maryland to eight NCAA championships and later built the University of Maryland, Baltimore County (UMBC), and the United States Naval Academy into competitive programs. Timchal's commitment to excellence and player development has made her a revered figure in women's lacrosse.

The Lacrosse Hall of Fame

The Lacrosse Hall of Fame, established in 1957 by US Lacrosse, honors individuals who have made significant contributions to the sport. Located in Sparks, Maryland, the Hall of Fame celebrates players, coaches, officials, and contributors who have shaped the history of lacrosse. Notable inductees include:

- Earle H. "Tommy" Thomason: One of the first great players in lacrosse history, Thomason was a standout at Johns Hopkins in the early 20th century. His skill and sportsmanship set the standard for future generations.

- Oren Lyons: A renowned Native American lacrosse player and advocate, Lyons played at Syracuse University and later became a prominent leader in the Iroquois Nationals lacrosse program. He is also a respected spiritual leader and activist for indigenous rights.

- Margery Fish: A pioneering figure in women's lacrosse, Fish was instrumental in the development of the sport in the United Kingdom. Her contributions to the game and her role in organizing international competitions have been vital to the growth of women's lacrosse.

- Jim Thorpe: An Olympic gold medalist and multi-sport athlete, Thorpe also excelled in lacrosse. His athleticism and versatility made him one of the most celebrated athletes of the early 20th century.

The contributions of iconic players and coaches have been instrumental in shaping the history and evolution of lacrosse. From trailblazing athletes like Jim Brown and Gary Gait to influential coaches like Dave Pietramala and Cindy Timchal, these individuals have left a lasting legacy on the sport. The Lacrosse Hall of Fame serves as a testament to their achievements and the enduring impact they have had on lacrosse. As we continue to explore the history of lacrosse, the stories of these legends inspire future generations to contribute to the growth and success of the sport.

LACROSSE AND POPULAR CULTURE

Lacrosse has made its mark not only on the field but also in popular culture, where it has influenced movies, television, literature, fashion, and lifestyle. This chapter delves into how lacrosse has been portrayed and celebrated in various media, its impact on fashion and lifestyle, and its role as a recreational and competitive activity for people of all ages.

Lacrosse in Movies, Television, and Literature

Lacrosse has appeared in various forms of entertainment, from Hollywood films to TV series and books, helping to raise the sport's profile and introduce it to broader audiences. Some notable examples include:

-   Movies: Lacrosse has been featured in several films, often highlighting its fast-paced and intense nature. One of the most notable films is "Crooked Arrows"

(2012), which tells the story of a Native American high school lacrosse team that competes in a prep school league. The film emphasizes the sport's cultural roots and the importance of heritage and teamwork.

- Television: Lacrosse has also made appearances on television, particularly in teen dramas and sports series. Shows like "Teen Wolf" (2011-2017) prominently featured lacrosse as the main sport played by the characters, showcasing the athleticism and excitement of the game. These portrayals have helped to popularize lacrosse among younger audiences.

- Literature: Lacrosse has been the subject of numerous books, both fiction and non-fiction. Authors have explored the sport's history, cultural significance, and the personal stories of players. Notable works include "Lacrosse: A History of the Game" by Donald M. Fisher and "The Spirit in the Stick" by Neil Duffy, which delve into the sport's rich heritage and its impact on individuals and communities.

The Influence of Lacrosse on Fashion and Lifestyle

Lacrosse's influence extends beyond the playing field, impacting fashion and lifestyle trends. The sport's unique culture and aesthetics have inspired various elements of style:

- Athleisure: The rise of athleisure fashion has seen lacrosse-inspired clothing become popular. Brands have created apparel that blends athletic functionality with casual style, including lacrosse jerseys, hoodies, and shorts. This trend has been embraced by both players and fans, making lacrosse gear a staple in everyday wear.

- Equipment Design: The design of lacrosse equipment, particularly sticks and protective gear, has evolved to become not only functional but also stylish. Players often customize their gear with unique colors and patterns, reflecting their personal style and team identity.

- Lifestyle Brands: Several lifestyle brands have emerged from the lacrosse community, offering products that cater to the sport's enthusiasts. These brands often emphasize the values of lacrosse, such as teamwork, perseverance, and respect for tradition, through their merchandise and marketing campaigns.

Lacrosse as a Recreational and Competitive Activity

Lacrosse's appeal as both a recreational and competitive sport has contributed to its growth at all levels of play. The sport offers opportunities for players of all ages and skill levels to engage in physical activity, develop their skills, and build camaraderie:

- Youth Leagues: Youth lacrosse leagues have proliferated across North America and beyond, providing young players with the chance to learn the game, compete in organized matches, and develop important life skills. These leagues often emphasize sportsmanship, teamwork, and fun, fostering a positive environment for children.

- High School and College Lacrosse: High school and college lacrosse have become highly competitive, with thousands of teams competing across various divisions. These levels of play offer a pathway for talented players to develop their skills, gain exposure, and potentially advance to professional or international competition.

- Adult and Masters Leagues: Lacrosse is not just for the young; adult and masters leagues offer opportunities for older players to continue enjoying the sport. These leagues cater to various skill levels and provide a social outlet for players to stay active and connected to the lacrosse community.

- Recreational Play: Beyond organized leagues, lacrosse is played recreationally in parks, beaches, and backyards around the world. Pickup games and informal practices allow players to enjoy the sport in a relaxed setting, fostering a love for the game that transcends competition.

Lacrosse's influence on popular culture, fashion, and lifestyle reflects its unique and enduring appeal. From its portrayal in movies and television to its impact on fashion trends and its role as a recreational activity, lacrosse has made a significant mark on society. As we continue to explore the history of lacrosse, it is clear that the sport's cultural footprint extends far beyond the field, inspiring and uniting people in diverse and meaningful ways.

THE BUSINESS OF LACROSSE

Lacrosse has evolved from its traditional roots into a sophisticated and commercially viable sport with significant economic impact. This chapter explores the business side of lacrosse, including the economics of professional and amateur leagues, the role of media rights and sponsorships, merchandising, and the emerging trends of fantasy lacrosse and sports betting.

The Economics of Professional and Amateur Lacrosse

The financial landscape of lacrosse encompasses both professional leagues and amateur organizations, each with its own economic structure and revenue streams:

- Professional Leagues: The growth of professional lacrosse leagues, such as the National Lacrosse League (NLL) and the Premier Lacrosse League (PLL), has introduced new economic opportunities. Revenue for these leagues primarily comes from ticket sales, broadcasting rights, sponsorship deals, and merchandise sales. The PLL, in particular, has adopted a tour-based model, bringing games to different cities across North America, which has helped to broaden its fan base and revenue potential.

- Player Salaries: Professional lacrosse players earn salaries that vary widely depending on the league, team, and individual player performance. While salaries in professional lacrosse are generally lower compared to other major sports, they have been steadily increasing as the sport grows in popularity and financial backing.

- Amateur and Collegiate Lacrosse: At the amateur level, lacrosse relies on funding from membership fees, donations, sponsorships, and support from educational institutions. High school and collegiate programs often benefit from school budgets, booster clubs, and community support. The NCAA Men's Lacrosse Championship and NCAA Women's Lacrosse Championship generate significant revenue through ticket sales, broadcasting rights, and sponsorships, which in turn support the sport's development at the collegiate level.

The Role of Media Rights and Sponsorships

Media rights and sponsorships play a crucial role in the

business of lacrosse, providing essential revenue streams and increasing the sport's visibility:

- Broadcasting Rights: The acquisition of broadcasting rights by major sports networks has been pivotal in promoting lacrosse. Networks like ESPN, NBC Sports, and CBS Sports have secured rights to broadcast professional and collegiate lacrosse games, reaching wider audiences and enhancing the sport's commercial appeal. These broadcasting deals bring in substantial revenue for leagues and teams.

- Sponsorship Deals: Sponsorships are another key revenue source, with companies eager to associate their brands with the dynamic and growing sport of lacrosse. Major sponsors include sports equipment manufacturers, apparel brands, and lifestyle companies. Sponsorship deals often include naming rights for events, advertising during broadcasts, and partnerships with players and teams for promotional campaigns.

Merchandising

Merchandising has become a significant aspect of the lacrosse business, encompassing the sale of equipment, apparel, and memorabilia:

- Equipment Sales: The demand for lacrosse

equipment, including sticks, helmets, gloves, and protective gear, drives a substantial portion of the sport's merchandise revenue. Leading brands like STX, Warrior, and Brine produce and market high-quality gear to players of all levels.

- Apparel: Lacrosse-themed apparel, such as jerseys, t-shirts, hoodies, and hats, is popular among players and fans alike. Official team merchandise, featuring professional and collegiate team logos, generates significant sales and helps to promote team identity and fan loyalty.

- Memorabilia: Collectibles and memorabilia, including autographed items, posters, and limited-edition gear, attract enthusiasts and collectors. These items often hold sentimental and monetary value, adding another dimension to the lacrosse merchandise market.

Fantasy Lacrosse and Sports Betting

The rise of fantasy sports and the legalization of sports betting in various regions have introduced new opportunities and challenges for lacrosse:

- Fantasy Lacrosse: Fantasy lacrosse leagues allow fans to create virtual teams composed of real players, earning points based on their performance in actual games. This interactive engagement increases fan interest and investment in the sport. Platforms like Fantrax and DraftKings have introduced fantasy lacrosse options, expanding the sport's digital presence.

- Sports Betting: The legalization of sports betting in several states and countries has opened new revenue streams for lacrosse. Betting on lacrosse games, including professional and collegiate matches, has become increasingly popular. Sportsbooks offer various betting options, such as moneyline bets, point spreads, and prop bets, attracting both seasoned bettors and casual fans. While sports betting presents economic opportunities, it also requires robust regulatory frameworks to ensure fairness and integrity in the sport.

The business of lacrosse has grown significantly, driven by professional leagues, media rights, sponsorships, merchandising, and emerging trends like fantasy sports and sports betting. These economic factors have not only provided essential revenue streams but also increased the sport's visibility and appeal. As lacrosse continues to evolve, its business landscape will likely see further growth and innovation, contributing to the sport's long-term success and sustainability. The commercial success of lacrosse highlights its potential as a major sport with a thriving economic ecosystem.

THE STORY OF LACROSSE

CONCLUSION

Lacrosse, often called "the fastest game on two feet," is more than just a sport; it is a vibrant and evolving cultural phenomenon with deep historical roots and a promising future. From its ancient beginnings among Native American tribes to its modern incarnation as a global sport, lacrosse has captivated and inspired countless individuals across generations and geographies.

Throughout this book, we have explored the multifaceted history of lacrosse, tracing its journey from the sacred fields of Native American culture to the professional arenas and international competitions of today. We have seen how the game was introduced to European settlers, how it evolved and formalized through the efforts of pioneers like Dr. William George Beers, and how it spread across Canada and the United States, eventually reaching a global audience.

We have also delved into the unique developments in women's lacrosse, the iconic players and coaches who have left an indelible mark on the sport, and the significant social issues that have shaped and been reflected in lacrosse. The business of lacrosse, with its burgeoning professional leagues, media rights, sponsorships, and merchandising, underscores the sport's growing economic impact and commercial viability.

As we look to the future, lacrosse faces both challenges and opportunities. The sport's continued expansion internationally, the integration of technology and data analytics, and the evolving landscape of societal attitudes and regulations will all play crucial roles in shaping its trajectory. Efforts to promote inclusivity, ensure player safety, and embrace sustainability will be essential for lacrosse to thrive in the modern era.

Lacrosse's enduring appeal lies in its dynamic gameplay, its deep cultural significance, and its ability to bring people together. It is a sport that embodies the values of teamwork, respect, and perseverance. As lacrosse continues to grow and evolve, it will undoubtedly inspire new generations of players and fans, building on its rich heritage and forging new traditions.

In conclusion, lacrosse is a testament to the power of sport to transcend boundaries, connect communities, and celebrate the human spirit. Its story is one of resilience, innovation, and passion, reflecting the diverse and dynamic world in which we live. As we celebrate the past and embrace the future, lacrosse remains a symbol of unity and excellence, a game that will continue to captivate and inspire for years to come.

APPENDIX

Glossary of Key Terms

- Attackman: A player whose primary responsibility is to score goals.
- Box Lacrosse: A version of lacrosse played indoors with fewer players and a smaller playing area.
- Crease: The circular area around the goal where only the goalie and defensive players can enter.
- Face-off: The method used to start play at the beginning of each quarter and after each goal, where two players contest for the ball.
- Field Lacrosse: The traditional outdoor version of lacrosse played with ten players on each team.
- Goalie (or Goaltender): The player who defends the goal.
- Ground Ball: When the ball is loose on the field and players attempt to gain possession.
- Midfielder: A player who plays both offense and defense, often running the length of the field.
- Penalty Box: The area where players serve time for committing penalties.
- Ride: The strategy used by the attacking team to prevent the defending team from clearing the ball from their defensive zone.
- Scoop: The technique of picking up a ground ball with the lacrosse stick.
- Stick Check: A defensive move where a player uses

their stick to try to knock the ball out of an opponent's stick.
- Transition: Moving the ball from the defensive end to the offensive end of the field.

Timeline of Key Events

- Pre-1600s: Lacrosse originates among Native American tribes in North America.
- 1630s: French Jesuit missionary Jean de Brébeuf documents the game among the Huron tribe.
- 1856: The Montreal Lacrosse Club is established.
- 1867: Dr. William George Beers codifies the first set of formal lacrosse rules.
- 1867: The National Lacrosse Association of Canada is founded.
- 1890: The first recorded women's lacrosse game is played at St. Leonard's School in Scotland.
- 1926: Rosabelle Sinclair establishes the first women's lacrosse team in the United States at the Bryn Mawr School.
- 1931: The Australian Lacrosse Association is formed.
- 1971: The first NCAA Men's Lacrosse Championship is held.
- 1982: The first NCAA Women's Lacrosse Championship is held.
- 1986: The National Lacrosse League (NLL) is founded.
- 2001: Major League Lacrosse (MLL) is founded.

- 2008: The Federation of International Lacrosse (FIL) is established.
- 2018: The Premier Lacrosse League (PLL) is launched.
- 2021: The Athletes Unlimited Lacrosse League is launched.

Further Reading and Watching

Books:
- Lacrosse: A History of the Game by Donald M. Fisher
- The Spirit in the Stick by Neil Duffy
- Tehokingáhsin: Great Things Will Happen by Jim Calder and Ron Fletcher
- Lacrosse Legends of the First Americans by Thomas Vennum
- The Creator's Game: A Story of Baaga'adowe/Lacrosse by Art Coulson

Articles and Journals:
- Journal of Sport History – various articles on the history and cultural significance of lacrosse.
- Native American Lacrosse: Little Brother of War by Thomas Vennum – an in-depth look at the origins and traditional aspects of lacrosse among Native American tribes.

Documentaries and Films:

- Crooked Arrows (2012) – A film about a Native American high school lacrosse team.
- Spirit Game: Pride of a Nation (2017) – A documentary exploring the cultural significance of lacrosse to the Iroquois Nationals.
- Keepers of the Game (2016) – A documentary about the challenges faced by a Native American girls' lacrosse team.
- The Medicine Game (2013) – A documentary following the lives of two brothers from the Onondaga Nation as they pursue their dreams of playing lacrosse.

Websites and Online Resources:
- US Lacrosse (www.uslacrosse.org) – The governing body for lacrosse in the United States, providing news, resources, and development programs.
- World Lacrosse (www.worldlacrosse.sport) – The international governing body for lacrosse, offering information on global competitions and development.
- Lacrosse All Stars (www.laxallstars.com) – A comprehensive site covering lacrosse news, gear reviews, and player development tips.
- Inside Lacrosse (www.insidelacrosse.com) – A leading source for lacrosse news, analysis, and recruiting information.

ABOUT THE AUTHOR

KJ Smith is a dedicated sports enthusiast and writer with a passion for uncovering the stories behind the games that captivate us. Known for their engaging storytelling and insightful analysis, KJ has written about a wide range of sports, diving into the histories, cultures, and personalities that shape them. *The Story of Lacrosse* is KJ's latest work, combining a love for athleticism with a talent for bringing lesser-known stories to light. Off the page, KJ can be found cheering from the sidelines, playing recreational sports, and inspiring readers to appreciate the beauty and dedication within every sport.

Made in the USA
Las Vegas, NV
19 December 2024